KU-466-940

*Mary Shelley* wrote one of the first great novels by a woman, a classic of Gothic literature: *Frankenstein*.

Born 30 August 1797, Mary was the daughter of two famous writers, William Godwin, a radical philosopher, and Mary Wollstonecraft, among whose writings was "A Vindication of the Rights of Woman". Mary Wollstonecraft died just eleven days after her daughter's birth.

As Mary grew older, she read in her parents' books of their dream of a world that would become more perfect as time passed, a place where all people could have equality, freedom and education, and she believed it possible too. Once her father remarried, however, he changed. His new wife didn't like Mary Wollstonecraft's ideas and didn't want young Mary to think like her.

Displeased with the friction between his daughter and his new wife, William Godwin sent fourteen-year-old Mary to Scotland, to live, until she was sixteen, with his friends the Baxters. Orphaned by her mother, spurned by her stepmother and sent away by her father, Mary was in need of company and affection. She found it at the Baxters' estate, high above the Firth of Tay.

The Scottish landscape, the tales her friends Isabel and Robert told and the warm family atmosphere had a lasting influence on Mary Shelley's life and art. In fact some believe that Mary's famous novel took root during those two important years. This is a fictionalized account of some of the events from that time.

# Through the Tempests

DUNDEE CITY COUNCIL

LOCATION
CC

ACCESSION NUMBER
COO 276 0707

SUPPLIER        PRICE
CYPHER          £12-99

CLASS No.       DATE
O15             12-3-03

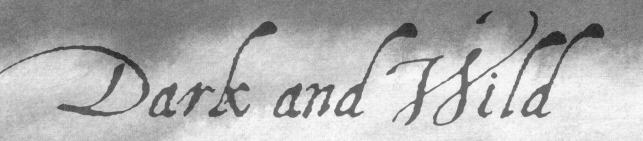

# Dark and Wild

## A Story of Mary Shelley

### Creator of Frankenstein

Sharon Darrow

illustrated by Angela Barrett

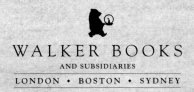

WALKER BOOKS
AND SUBSIDIARIES

LONDON • BOSTON • SYDNEY

*s a wave receded,* Mary reached into its wake and grabbed a shell tumbling in the surf.

"Isabel," she called. "Come and see this one."

Isabel splashed across the wet sand, her older brother, Robert, running behind her. Isabel took the pink and yellow coiled shell from Mary's hand. "It's lovely."

"Look at these." Robert held out three tiny, horn-shaped shells. Mary touched the smallest, most delicate one.

"That one's for you, Mary," Robert said. "And here's one for you, Isabel." He put the third in his own pocket. "One for each of us."

Mary, Robert, and Isabel walked arm in arm towards the dune path. On the narrow incline, Robert pulled away, swung his arms out wide and said, "I'll catch you if you fall."

"And who is it that'd be stumbling three times on his way down?" Isabel said.

Mary laughed. "And who was it Isabel and I had to pull from the sea yesterday when his sailing boat took on water?"

Robert hummed a mournful hymn, then grinned. "And who is eternally grateful?"

Just then, Mary's foot slipped and Robert's hand steadied her. She smiled.

Eternally grateful was what Mary was. It hadn't been easy, being sent away by her father and sailing to Scotland to live with strangers. Seasickness had plagued her. And homesickness. But after nearly two years with the Baxters, Mary's yearning for London had waned. The Cottage was a warm, safe haven, a home like the one she might have had if her mother had lived and if her father had not abandoned both his beliefs and Mary.

*In the evenings,* Isabel, Robert and Mary often gathered before the fire and took turns telling stories. Mary loved to retell the epic tales and poems she'd heard recited in her family's parlour by many of the famous writers in England, such as Samuel Taylor Coleridge.

When she recited his poem *The Rime of the Ancient Mariner*, the spectres of lost sailors seemed to creep into the shadows and twist through the folds of the draperies on the tall dark windows. In the darkest corner of the room, a tiny tongue of reflected firelight became the glittering eye of the cursed mariner.

> "The many men so beautiful!
> And they all dead did lie:
> And a thousand thousand slimy things
> Lived on; and so did I."

Robert liked legends of heroes and of monsters like Glaslich, a giant who was said to haunt the craggy coast. And Isabel always chose ghostly tales.

One night, as the wind moaned down the chimney, Isabel put her finger to her lips and said, "Hush now, and I'll tell you the true story of a lonely lass whose lover, a sailor, had drowned in the North Sea."

Robert and Mary leaned closer.

ON A MOONLIT SUMMER NIGHT, when
all the village lads and lasses gathered at the crossroads
to dance and court and make merry, one sorrowful lass crept
along behind and hid in the hedgerow. Her poor grieving
heart couldn't join in the merriment and the dancing.

"On this night a stranger rode in through the mist, leapt
from his horse and danced the evening gone. His cape
always hid his face, but there was something about the man
that reminded the lass of her lost love, and she wept all the
more for watching him.

"So distracted was she with weeping and sighing alone
in the shadows that she hardly noticed the others departing.
Finally, only she remained at the darkened crossroads — only
she and the shadowy stranger.

"He approached her. 'Why do you weep, sweet lass?'
And throwing back his hood, he asked, 'Is this not the face of
the one you long for?'

"The lass fell into her lover's arms. 'Are you yet alive?'
She wiped her tears and the sailor scooped her up into his
arms and carried her to his horse. They rode through the

night towards his seaside home, the lass, holding tight to his waist, happy once more.

"They galloped away from the approaching dawn and into the dark of the west. It occurred to the lass that her sailor was in a hurry to return to the sea, to the shore of his beloved sea. But as they galloped on, the lass grew tired. 'Do stop and rest for a while, my love,' she begged. But it was as if he hadn't heard a word.

"Then a strange thing happened. The sailor's cape grew damp. At first the lass thought it was raining, but she felt not a drop. Or maybe, she thought, the heavy mist of the inland village had soaked his clothing. But no, her own had stayed dry except for the spots of her tears.

"The closer they rode to the sea, the wetter her sailor's clothing became. And beneath her grasp, she felt his strong waist grow thin, a most unhealthy thinness. Not like her lover at all.

"'Who are you?' she cried, as he turned the horse toward a lonely kirkyard.

"The man dragged her off the horse, clutching her close. He threw back his hood once more and, in place of her dear lover's face, only a pale skull remained. 'You say you love me,' he scolded, 'yet your grief has kept me from my rest all these seven months. Now you will come to my low and narrow house and we will be together always, as is your dearest wish! We must hurry — the sun is arising.'

"Dawn tinted the eastern sky. The lass's old love pulled her into the kirkyard, her tartan shawl held fast in his grip. She struggled, slipped from her shawl and fell to the earth. As the first rays shot through the nearby wood, the man

stepped onto his grave and vanished. Only a tiny, fringed corner of the shawl now showed above ground. Seeing that the rest was buried deep in the sod, as if undisturbed for all these months, the lass fainted.

"Revived hours later by the vicar and the grave-digger, she tugged at her shawl but could not release it from the grasp of the earth. The grave-digger dug around it, down and down until all but the last corner was free. Still they couldn't pull it from the grave.

"'Dig deeper,' said the vicar. But when the shovel entered the sod again, it struck something hard — the bony fingers of the ghostly sailor, still clutching the edge of the tartan shawl."

In the quiet room, Mary, Robert and Isabel watched a log break and settle into the coals of the grate.

"Will you tell us a story now, Mary?" Robert asked.

Mary shivered and said, "Yes, I shall tell you about another lost love. During a stormy summer sixteen years ago, a great comet rose over London..."

*A* MAN AND A WOMAN, *deeply in love, were soon to have their first child. After many cloudy nights, the sky finally cleared. As the comet streaked across the rooftops of London, their baby girl was born. They thought this meant she was blessed by the heavens and called the comet their child's 'own bright star'. But soon the storms returned and the mother grew ill. She died when the baby was only eleven days old.*

*"The father grieved. Many days all he could do was sit beside his true love's grave, inconsolable.*

*"He named his daughter after his wife, Mary, and taught her to read her name from the gravestone. As the girl grew older, her visits to St Pancras churchyard grew more frequent. Beneath the weeping willows, her mother's spirit comforted her and assured her that she was loved. Even when she found friends and a home far away the little churchyard waited, ready to reunite her with the one soul she would forever miss and would never know in this world."*

When Mary finished her story, she said, "If my mother had lived, I am certain my father would not have forgotten all he and my mother believed and wrote about in their books."

In the last glow of firelight, Mary said, "My father used to tell me that a person 'who is afraid to think unlike others, will soon learn not to think at all.'"

*Late the next day,* the Baxters set up their easels on the lawn, as they did on many afternoons in good weather, and painted the sea and the dunes. Mary didn't want to draw the waves or try to capture the light on the beach — or even to paint a wild rose or a foraging bird as she had done at home on Hampstead Heath. Not with the memory of the story she'd told the night before still heavy in her heart.

Mary called out, "I'll be in the pine grove."

She loved to sit in the deep shade in the hills behind the house, soothed by the sigh of the pines, and write stories. Today she stayed for a long time, brooding and staring at the ruins of a castle on a rocky point. Sprays of surf plumed up around it, the rhythmic waves faint in the distance.

Mary took up her pen and began a new story. This story was set in Scotland with echoes of the haunted tales and legends of its people, whispers of moor and mountain eyrie, and the chill of the North Sea.

Twilight fell across the Firth of Tay, the Baxters gathered up their paint boxes and Robert called to Mary to come indoors.

As they entered The Cottage, Mrs Baxter picked up a letter from the table by the door. "A letter from your father," she said, and handed it to Mary.

Mary followed the Baxters into the parlour, her heart pounding.

As dusk deepened around the quiet house, Mary and the Baxters settled into their chairs. Mr Baxter read from the Bible and Mrs Baxter stitched a tapestry, nodding now and again when her husband read a passage aloud. Isabel embroidered a tiny white rosebud in the corner of a linen handkerchief and Robert curled up in front of the fire with the cat and a book. They all feigned unconcern as they waited for Mary to read her letter.

*My dear Mary,*

*I have decided you may return home. Now that you have broadened your education, I desire that you no longer burden the Baxters, but return to M. J. Godwin & Co.*

*I trust you will have sufficiently matured to rejoin the household as a temperate young woman, ready to help with the manuscripts in the publishing house. Mr Baxter has assured me you have caused no disharmony but have conducted yourself with prudence and contentment.*

*Your loving Papa*

Mary folded the letter.

Isabel looked up. "Good news, Mary?"

"I'm to return home."

Robert sat up. "That's not good news."

At that moment Mary could imagine staying for ever, but said, "Papa needs me."

"Of course," said Mrs Baxter. "Your father must certainly miss you. And your duty is to your family."

The time had finally come when Mary's father wanted her back home — in fact, needed her. She would return to London and make him proud. She'd be a better daughter, work hard and never argue with her stepmother or her brothers and sisters again.

"I will miss you, but I'll come back again someday," Mary said. "And you can visit me in London."

That night, their stories by the fireside weren't about ghosts or heroes, but of their walks by the sea, afternoons of sailing, canters on horseback through the surf, family trips to the mountains and hikes across high glaciers that felt like the top of the world.

Robert said, "I'll never forget you, Mary."

Mary cut a long wavy lock of her bright auburn hair, wrapped it in a green ribbon and gave it to Isabel. Isabel cut a lock of her own, plaited it through with crimson yarn and handed it to Mary.

"With these remembrances," Isabel said, "we vow our friendship will never end."

*On the morning* of her return voyage, Mary awoke before first light, restless and unhappy. How could she bear to leave Scotland and the Baxters? She stood at her bedroom window as dawn lit the snowy peaks of the Grampian Mountains, and the loneliness of her life in London returned—the noise, the bickering, and her father's constant worry about money. Mary wished the peace of the Baxter household could travel with her to her family's house on Skinner Street. Remembering her seasickness on the ten-day voyage two years ago, Mary held her stomach and crawled back into bed. Before her final day in Scotland began, she dreamed a last melancholy dream...

A HOWLING *came over the moor*
*beneath a yellow moon.*
*The people barred their doors,*
*hid under the eiderdowns*
*and tried their best to sleep.*
*For a lonely ghost wandered the north,*
*peering into windows as she passed.*
*At last she reached Scotland and climbed*
*the highest mountain peak,*
*then descended to walk by the sea,*
*forever choosing shells*
*to leave on the doorsteps of all*
*those she had ever loved,*
*hoping they would never forget*
*that they had once loved her.*

*At the first sight* of the *Osnaburgh,* the Baxters' friends and
family gathered round. "Farewell, Mary," they called.

Isabel took Mary's hand. "Don't forget our vow. If ever we need
each other, we'll be there."

"Always." Mary hugged Isabel and turned towards the sea.

The servants carried her trunk down the steep path to the beach.
Robert, who had hardly spoken all morning, followed Mary.
Halfway down, she threw her arms out, tried to laugh, and called
over her shoulder, "Don't worry, Robert. If you stumble, I'll
catch you."

"And I'll be eternally grateful, too," Robert said, his voice sad.

Robert and Mr Baxter rowed Mary out to the *Osnaburgh*. Robert helped her board the ship. When it was time to release her hand, Robert held it a moment longer and said, "I'll come to London soon."

"I'll be there," Mary said.

The steamer began its slow turn from shore. Back on the beach, Mr Baxter and Robert joined the others waving goodbye. In one hand Mary clasped the tiny shell Robert had given her, in the other, the lock of Isabel's hair. She watched until the thin line of the shore disappeared.

Alone now and empty as the horizon, Mary wept.

The waves swelled as the *Osnaburgh* passed from the Firth of Tay into open water. Seasickness rolled over Mary, and by the time they docked in London ten days later, she could barely lift her head.

Mary's father rushed to greet her. In his arms, his woollen waistcoat smelling of ink and rough against her cheek, Mary, weak and stiff from the journey, relaxed.

He smiled at her and said, "You are more like your mother than ever, and your voice so like hers it almost makes me weep." At that moment, Mary loved her father more than anyone else on earth. "But I won't weep today," he continued. "I'll rejoice in your safe return."

Mary linked her arm through his. Home at last. Now, perhaps, her life would be as she had always imagined.

In the coach, her father sighed. "There's so much to do at the publishing house. You can help with the writing, editing and correspondence."

Mary smiled. "I already have some ideas for stories."

"Good," her father said.

Mary settled back against the seat, steady again with solid ground under her feet and her father wanting her to work by his side.

As the coach lurched forward, her father said, "I have urgent business that will often call me away from home. You couldn't have returned at a better time to help your second mamma."

A wave ran through Mary, the seasickness returning and with it the image of the lonely castle crumbling into the North Sea.

*In the family's rooms* above the publishing house, the arguments between Mary and her stepmother returned. Mary couldn't read or write fast enough. She wouldn't dress the way her stepmother wished, but persisted in wearing the tartan dresses she had worn in Scotland as a way of feeling closer to Isabel and Robert. She didn't help her half-sister, Fanny, with the housekeeping. She didn't praise stepsister Jane's playing and singing enough.

"You are just like your mother," her stepmother said, "shamefully proud, bold and headstrong! You think of no one except yourself."

Mary wished she were more like her mother — strong and

courageous, a woman who knew what she believed and was willing to suffer for it. Maybe then her stepmother's anger wouldn't bother her so much. Maybe then her father's frequent absences to solicit loans from friends to pay his debts, and the way he drooped at his desk when he was home, wouldn't make Mary feel as far away from him as if she were still in Scotland.

Even when her father was home and she resumed her studies with him, trouble arose. She wanted to study Greek like her brothers, Charles and William, and the other young scholars who visited her father, but he said, "A woman doesn't need both Greek and Latin."

*Now Mary was lonelier* than she had ever been. She missed the Baxters, their circle of friends, Scotland's ice-covered mountains, and the stories of magnificent warriors and sad lovers always destined to part. Mary longed for the peace of her room at The Cottage and her retreat in the pine grove. But even more, Mary longed for someone who could see into her heart and mind.

Mary went to the parlour and sat beneath her mother's portrait. With a quiet resolve she'd not felt before, Mary dipped her pen in the inkwell and continued the story she had begun in the pine grove. A story of pride and sorrow, loneliness and lost love, fear and despair — and in the face of it all, a heroine filled with hope, struggling for the courage to be true to herself and to tell her story.

# Afterword

One day early in May, only five weeks after she had left Scotland, Mary sat in the parlour translating Virgil's *Aeneid* when a young philosopher-poet, Percy Bysshe Shelley, arrived to study with her father. Mary and Shelley quickly became friends and met secretly in St Pancras churchyard under the willows at Mary's mother's grave. Not long after, Robert Baxter came to London to ask Mary to marry him and return to Scotland and The Cottage. But it was too late. Mary was in love with Shelley. On 28 July, Mary and Shelley, who was already married, eloped to Europe; Mary was not quite seventeen years old. They travelled across the Alps by mule cart and sailed down the Rhine, mooring their boat under the ruins of a castle belonging to a noble family by the name of Frankenstein.

When they returned to London, Mary's father and stepmother were so angry they refused to see her. And Isabel's new husband, shocked by Mary and Shelley's scandalous behaviour, wouldn't allow Isabel to answer Mary's letters.

Mary and Percy's first child, a daughter, was born early and lived only a few days. Six nights later, Mary had a dream and wrote in her journal: "Dream that my little baby came to life again – that it

"It was a dreary night of November, that I beheld the accomplishment of my toils."
Viktor Frankenstein

had only been cold & that we rubbed it by the fire & it lived — I awake & find no baby — I think about the little thing all day." Of their three other children, only one son lived to adulthood.

Mary's deep emotional responses to her life experiences are sure to have influenced her fiction. Her mother's death in childbirth, the estrangement from her father, the need for someone to love her and the death of her own baby were all elements that played into the shaping of the story of Frankenstein. Even such things as being banned from her father's Greek lessons and eavesdropping as he taught the young scholars may have consciously or unconsciously influenced the creation of such scenes as those of Frankenstein's monster eavesdropping on the cottagers in order to learn language.

Mary Shelley finished writing *Frankenstein* at just nineteen. Some people in Scotland say she began her story in the pine grove near The Cottage on the Firth of Tay. But Mary said the idea for *Frankenstein* came from a dream she had after an evening spent reading ghost stories before a roaring fire in Lord Byron's villa on a lake in the Alps, a night that reminded her of her time in Scotland and the tales Robert and Isabel told. Amid lightning and thunder, Lord Byron's guests challenged one another to write ghostly tales even more frightening than those they had read.

Mary said that when she lay her head on her pillow a few nights later: "My imagination, unbidden, possessed and guided me ... I saw the pale student of unhallowed arts kneeling beside the thing he had put together. I saw the hideous phantasm of a man stretched out, and then, on the working of some powerful engine, show signs of life."

The day after her scary dream, Mary began writing her famous story in the voice of Viktor Frankenstein:

*It was a dreary night of November, that I beheld the accomplishment of my toils. With an anxiety that almost amounted to agony, I collected the instruments of life around me, that I might infuse a spark of being into the lifeless thing that lay at my feet. It was already one in the morning; the rain pattered dismally against the panes, and my candle was nearly burnt out, when, by the glimmer of the half-extinguished light, I saw the dull yellow eye of the creature open; it breathed hard, and a convulsive motion agitated its limbs.*

The first book of science fiction, *Frankenstein, or The Modern Prometheus*, has inspired many other books, plays, films and even cartoons. Published anonymously in 1817, *Frankenstein* became an

immediate success. Mary became a romantic heroine to some, though others disliked her because of her father's progressive philosophies, her mother's ideas about women and Mary's own relationship with Shelley. Some hated her book and wanted to ban or censor it because of its underlying criticism of society's move toward industrialization and increasing dependence on science at the expense of the human spirit.

When Mary was only twenty-four years old, Percy Bysshe Shelley drowned off the coast of Italy. Her dedication to his memory lasted all her life. She compiled and edited his life's work and made sure his reputation as a great poet grew as the years passed.

Some of Mary Shelley's works were unpublished or lost, but among those published are novels, plays, stories, poems, translations and adaptations, travel books, biographies, articles and reviews and books for children.

Isabel Baxter was Mary's first real friend, and after Shelley's death the two resumed their friendship. When Mary died, on 1 February 1851, her son, Percy, sent a lock of his mother's hair to Isabel in Scotland.

Now, two hundred years after her birth, people all over the world have heard of Mary Shelley, the creator of Frankenstein's monster.

*Thou Friend, whose presence on my wintry heart*
*Fell, like Spring upon some herbless plain*
Percy Bysshe Shelley

❧

To the memory of Mary Shelley and Mary Wollstonecraft,
and, in gratitude, to Mary Lee Donovan
S. D.

First published 2003 by Walker Books Ltd
87 Vauxhall Walk, London SE11 5HJ

2 4 6 8 10 9 7 5 3 1

Text © 2003 Sharon Darrow
Illustrations © 2003 Angela Barrett

This book has been typeset in Phaistos

Printed in Hong Kong

All rights reserved. No part of this book may be reproduced, transmitted
or stored in an information retrieval system in any form or by any means, graphic,
electronic or mechanical, including photocopying, taping and recording,
without prior written permission from the publisher.

British Library Cataloguing in Publication Data:
a catalogue record for this book
is available from the British Library

ISBN 0-7445-5664-3